Eucharistic Sacrifice:

The Roots of a

Metaphor

by

Rowan Williams

Lecturer in Divinity University of Cambridge
Canon Theologian, Leicester Cathedral

GROVE BOOKS

BRAMCOTE   NOTTS. NG9 3DS

CONTENTS

THE COVER PICTURE

shows the sarcifices of Abel, Noah, and Melchisedek, as shown on a building at Ravenna in Italy, and its use was inspired by a similar print in *The Study of Liturgy* (S.P.C.K., London, 1978) p.228, and permitted by the owners of the print, the Mansell Collection.

FOREWORD

This study had its beginnings when I was asked to present a 'Catholic' response to Professor Hanson's earlier Study, *Eucharistic Offering in the Early Church*.[1] As things turned out, I found little impulse to attempt a refutation of Professor Hanson's impeccably documented survey; I had more interest in suggesting other perspectives on, and other possible developments from, the sacrificial imagery of early Christianity. So the present essay, while it has its points of disagreement with Professor Hanson, can be read as complementary rather than contradictory (I hope).

By no stretch of the imagination could I be called a professional liturgiologist, but I am fortunate in my friends. Bryan Spinks and Kenneth Stevenson have both supplied and suggested useful material, and generally have saved me from too many downright ignorant blunders. The Rev. David Rayner, of Great St. Mary's, Cambridge, and Dr. Sebastian Brock of Oxford helped me interpret some of the Syrian material touched on here (my Syriac is rudimentary; translations are heavily indebted to the Latin of the nineteenth century editors and the German of Dom Edmund Beck). My love and thanks to all of them.

Rowan Williams
July, 1982

[1] R. P. C. Hanson *Eucharistic Offering in the Early Church* (Grove Liturgical Study no. 19, Grove Books, 1979).

First Impression September 1982

ISSN 0306—0608

ISBN 0 907536 32 8

1. INTRODUCTION

Objections to the use of sacrificial language in eucharistic theology seem to crystallize in three main areas. First, and most obviously, there is the classical Reformation objection that any hint of the eucharist being *a* sacrifice fatally compromises the *ephapax* of the letter to the Hebrews; it undermines the all-sufficiency of the cross and so removes the ground of Christian assurance, Hence Professor Hanson's rejection of any 'anxious nagging in our faith and its practice'[1]; if eucharistic sacrifice suggests that we are obliged constantly to petition God to act for our salvation, as if he had not already done so, it is 'a confession of lack of faith'.[2] Calvin in his fine commentary on Hebrews accepts the Catholic point that the eucharist is not a new sacrifice or in any sense independent of Calvary; he is far too intelligent a polemicist to direct his shafts at any vulgar distortions of the doctrine. But even if the eucharist is merely a kind of 'activation' of the grace of Calvary for the healing of present sinfulness, the implication is that the *past* sacrifice of Christ has not removed the consciousness of sin in Christians: like the sacrifices of the old Law it is 'weak' *because* it needs re-presentation. 'The apostle . . . teaches that the sacrifices of the Law were abolished by the death of Christ because there was remembrance of sins in them. It is clear from this that this kind of application [of Christ's sacrifice] which they [the Catholics] invent has disappeared'.[3]

Calvin is worth quoting because, as so often, he goes swiftly to the heart of the question; and in his discussion he raises implicitly not only the whole question of the doctrine of assurance but the second focus of objection, which is to do with who is the *agent* in the eucharist. If Christ's sacrifice needs 'activation', this suggests that Christ is not now mighty to save by and through his accomplished work. It is he and he alone who pleads his sacrifice: 'Christ is continually doing this because he rose from the dead for this purpose'.[4] He is throughout agent and initiator, never passive; he is not an object in the church's life and worship, but always subject—personal, free, alive, and active. Doctrines of eucharistic sacrifice transfer the agency to church or priest and thus immobilize Christ. Paradoxically, by insisting on the need for a making present of Calvary, they underline the purely historical pastness of the cross, abstracting it from its place in the eternal priestly life of Christ, who is, as risen and glorified, ceaselessly active for our salvation.

And this leads logically into the third area of complaint, stressed by Professor Hanson[5] as by so many theologians in rhe Reformed tradition. If the

---

[1] R. P. C. Hanson *Eucharistic Offering in the Early Church* (Grove Liturgical Study no. 19, Grove Books, 1979) p.29.

[2] *Ibid.*

[3] Calvin on Hebrews 10.15 *(Calvin's Commentaries: The Epistle of Paul the Apostle to the Hebrews and the First and Second Epistles of St. Peter,* tr. by W. B. Johnston (T. and T. Clark, Edinburgh, 1963) p.139 (and cf. p.133)).

[4] *Ibid.,* p.101 (on Hebrews 5.25).

[5] *Op. cit.,* pp.18, 24-26; and *Christian Priesthood Examined* (Mowbray, London, 1979), pp.55-59, 79-80, 95-99.

agency of Christ is transferred to the church and the church exercises this agency at the hands of the clergy, the way is open for the development of radically sub-Christian or anti-Christian understanding of ministry. The ordained Christian is seen as exercising a 'priesthood' different in kind from that of the whole company of the baptized, a 'priesthood' deriving from Christ through the apostles, somehow mirroring in more direct fashion the mediatorial and transforming and interpretative role of Christ. Thus the language of eucharistic sacrifice provides the ideological grounding for a strongly hierarchical understanding of the relation of ministers and laity. The priest as custodian of holy things, equipped with supernatural power and privileged access to the resources of the invisible world, is in a position to enforce sanctions of ultimate weight—as in mediaeval Christendom. Sacramental power guarantees the right to determine unilaterally the limits of the Christian community.

All in all, this constitutes a weighty indictment. It touches on fundamental matters of belief to do with the exercise of power, the accessibility to all of 'the holy' in Christian understanding, and the individual and collective self-images of the redeemed. What is being argued is that 'eucharistic sacrifice' represents a far-reaching paganization of Christianity. It is more than the familiar question of our having nothing in our own right worthy to be offered to God; it is a forcing of the Christian gospel back into the 'history of religions', undermining the truth that the whole story of Christ, and of his death especially, is the crucial intersection of history and eternity. Calvary is not repeatable, in a sense it is not even *representable*. There is no 'thing' there, no mere memory or narrative to be applied to distant times and places; but because it happened in our world, God's grace is free in our world, free to act now to heal and save us.

I have emphasized this aspect of the debate because I am aware that some Catholic defenders of 'eucharistic sacrifice' language have given in to the temptation to caricature the Reformed doctrine as if it implied that our present salvation were a long-range effect of an event in the past. It is, in fact, quite clear from the arguments of Calvin and others[1] that the basic theological premise in the classical Reformed thesis is the eternal saving agency of Christ, which never needs to be 'reawakened' or 'applied' by human agents. It is without qualification free, sovereign, and effective, because of Calvary: in other words it has as much scope, as much power, in our world as it can have. It is not somehow veiled or locked up unless and until eucharistically enacted.

---

[1] See for instance, Jewel's *Reply to Harding's Answer* (in vol. 1 of *The Works of John Jewel, Bishop of Salisbury*; ed. for the Parker Society by John Ayre, Cambridge, 1845), p.128:

> 'Likewise the same one sacrifice is everlasting, not only in itself, for that the virtue thereof is daily effectual in us, and endureth forever; but also on our behalf, in that we do daily offer up unto God our sacrifices of praises and thanksgiving for that so merciful and wonderful work of our redemption . . . Thus is that sacrifice once offered upon the cross rightly called our daily sacrifice.'

Jewel is clear that Christ's eternal priesthood means that he is eternally active through his sacrifice on Calvary.

There is constant need in this weary controversy to go back to such basic premises. Canon Leslie Houlden has well said that the problem with 'most of the commonest formulations involving sacrificial language is that they start too far up the conceptual ladder; that is, they presuppose more fundamental theological concepts which seem not to be fully clear, like a mountain whose summit is exposed while the lower levels are shrouded in mist'.[1]

My purpose in the reflections that follow will be to argue that there are ways of handling the language of sacrifice in relation to the eucharist and the church at large which do justice to the central concern for the priority of Christ's agency—ways of speaking with some quite extensive roots in early Christian tradition; and I hope too to suggest why so many of my fellow-Catholics find that a eucharistic theology which entirely brackets the question of sacrifice is an impoverishment not only of sacramental theology but of the whole range of our understanding of salvation and the redeemed life. In other words, I hope to explore some of the mist-shrouded lower levels rather than concentrating on the supposed clarities of the visible summit. The ramifications of the issues touched on are enormously wide, and I can do no more than sketch some areas for further reflection; but I believe that some thematic unities will emerge fairly plainly.

---

[1] 'Sacrifice and the Eucharist', in *Explorations in Theology,* London, 1978, p.80 (originally in *Thinking about the Eucharist,* ed. I. T. Ramsey (S.C.M., London, 1972)).

2. FROM APOLOGETIC TO THEOLOGY—
THE SECOND CENTURY

One of the salient facts about early Christianity which we easily overlook was its external irreligiousness. The popular Roman charge of 'atheism' is part of a general sense in late antiquity that Christians had no tangible public forms of piety. They operate in secrecy, so that, notoriously, their ritual behaviour is more like the oaths of secret societies than the corporate cultus of rational civic human beings living openly in the *polis*.[1] And because sacrifice was something so entirely fundamental to religious practice in the ancient world, the Christians' non-participation in sacrifice is a mark of their alienation from ordinary human piety, their rejection of *custom*[2]—both Jewish and Gentile tradition. Christians are disturbingly private people, whose very existence ruptures the harmony of the *polis*. The state has its civic ritual and sacrifice, and under that umbrella various subsidiary kinds of sacrificial and cultic activity may go on in smaller groups; but the church not only refuses to come under this umbrella, but practises no traditional rites itself. Thus it can only exist for itself its rites (whether or not they are the abominations reported by hostile gossip) promote not the harmony of heaven and earth but the cohesion of the group: their spiritual power is not answerable to the welfare of the public world, and so is quasi-magical.[3]

Not sacrificing, then, is part of a whole complex of ideas and attitudes perceived as hostile by the intelligent pagan. There is no problem—for a Celsus, an Iamblichus, or a Julian—about the gods being angry if not propitiated: they and their like have long been critical of any such crude account of sacrifice and the divine.[4] But they *are* worried about the up-setting of a delicate overall balance expressed in traditional rites: the church represents almost a 'secularized' kind of religious activity, because its spiritual power is privately operated.[5] So a very important part of the Christian apologist's task, in the second century especially, is to demon-strate that Christianity is not hostile to tradition and cult, neither is it indifferent to the public realm. Examples could be multiplied; but we shall concentrate on the defensive points made in connection with sacrifice. Part of the agenda for an apologist will be to show both that Christianity accepts the sophisticated Greek attitude to sacrifice (it is not a blood-offering to buy off an angry deity) and the propriety of sacrificial language and practice; and also that the Christian cult is not invention or innovation. If we have these goals in mind, it may be easier to understand the very fluid language of second-century writers about Christian sacrifice.

1 Origen, *Contra Celsum* I. 1-3; compare the '*sacramentum*' of Pliny's Epp. X. 96.
2 E.g. *Contra Celsum* V. 33-44. For an excellent general discussion of these and other passages, see Frances Young, *The Use of Sacrificial Ideas in Greek Christian Writers from the New Testament to John Chrysostom.* (Cambridge, Mass. 1979) ch. IV. *passim.*
3 On the late antique preoccupation with the locus of spiritual power and the importance of 'socializing' its exercise, see Peter Brown *The Making of Late Antiquity* (Harvard and London, 1978).
4 Young, *op. cit.,* pp.15-34.
5 There is a classical account of Christianity's subversion of civic piety in N. D. Fustel de Coulanges, *The Ancient City* (Gloucester, Mass., 1979—a reprint of Willard Small's 1873 translation).

The 'pure offering' tradition, looking back to Malachi 1.11, presents an extremely fruitful controversial strategy. Some strands of thinking in Hellenistic Judaism (Philo, Aristeas) had already moved some way towards an equivalence of prayer and sacrifice, or simply virtuous life and sacrifice,[1] and early Christian writers were always happy to exploit the 'obedience is better than sacrifice' tradition of certain parts of the Old Testament. Irenaeus gives perhaps the most detailed discussion of such scriptural passages[2], but Justin also alludes to them.[3] Athenagoras[4], although his direct quotation in this connection comes from Homer, obviously has Old Testament texts like Psalm 50 at the back of his mind in countering the Homeric picture of votive offerings to turn away divine displeasure, and uses the phrase employed by Paul in Romans 12.1, *logike latreia,* ('reasonable' or 'logical' service), the worship of the reasoning spirit. 'Rational' and 'bloodless' worship, which for Athenagoras is primarily thankful acknowledgment of God as creator, does the job of sacrifice—which is not specified directly in the text, but may be assumed from the context to have something to do with the life of 'the cities'[5] (the reference to sin-offering in the Homeric quotation is obviously not central for Athenagoras). Like other apologists, Athenagoras is careful to insist that Christians pray for the state[6], and that their lives are harmonious in terms both of civic relationships and of the bond between earth and heaven. Presumably, the idea of virtue and thanksgiving as sacrificial finds its place here. What do Christians do for the *polis*? Answer, they 'sacrifice' by their reasonable worship and upright life.

This cluster of ideas, in short, represents a riposte to the charge that Christians manipulate spiritual power for private, not civic, ends. It leaves unanswered the problem of the apparent absence of visible sacrifice and cult. Justin, however, manages to kill several birds with one stone when he describes to Trypho the significance of the eucharist.[7] It is prefigured in the cleansed leper's offering of meal (Lev. 14.10) and prophesied by Malachi in the familiar words about the 'pure offering'. Thus Christian cultus is not novel and untraditional: now that the temporary injunctions of the Law are abolished, the hidden purposes of God are manifest, and it is clear from the text of the Mosaic regulations that God foresaw their decisive fulfilment and conclusion in Christ and his church.[8] They are not *meant* to last, so Christians cannot be held guilty for abandoning Jewish tradition: on the contrary, it is they who observe the original and deepest sense of the Mosaic Law. Furthermore, here is a recognizable cultic act, in which bread and wine are *offered* ritually as a memorial and a thanksgiving[9]: while it is true that prayer and thanksgiving are the only real

1 Young, *op. cit.,* pp.64-66; R. Daly, S.J., *The Origins of the Christian Doctrine of Sacrifice* (London and Philadelphia, 1978) pp.104-110 (on Philo).
2 *Adversus Haereses* IV. 17 and 18.
3 *Dialogue* 22.
4 *Legatio.* 13. 2-4; on the phrase, rational and bloodless', cf. infra, note 5, p.13 for its roots in Hellenistic Judaism.
5 *Ibid.* 13.1, 14.1.
6 *Ibid.* 11, 2-3, 37.2.
7 *Dialogue* 41.
8 *Ibid.* 40.
9 Cf. *ibid.* 117, *Apol.* 1.65-67.

sacrifices, the ritual form of this for Christians is the 'sacrifice' of food and drink so as to remember the passion of Jesus.[1] All Christian thanksgiving is made in relation to the saving death of Christ.

There is no doubt for Justin that the eucharist is 'structurally' a sacrifice— as indeed it would have looked to the uninitiated observer. His point is a fairly simple one, in fact: Christianity conceives of itself as a normal and acceptable and traditional form of piety, i.e. as sacrificial; and although it has no mythological fantasies about propitiatory sacrifice and its necessity, although it accepts the Jewish and Greek convention of seeing 'true' sacrifice as interior and spiritual, it acknowledges the dependence of our capacity for true worship upon the saving death of Christ, and it does so— natually—by memorializing the death of Christ in the way he enjoined, by offering up and sharing bread and wine, So we have a spiritual understanding of sacrifice *and* a sacrificial rite. The flank is neatly turned against the various forms of accusation of 'atheism'—and, incidentally, the universalist thrust of Malachi 1.11 speaks against any 'privatizing' understanding of the context and function of Christian worship.

By linking the understanding of spiritual sacrifice firmly to Christ's death, Justin has gone a little further than Athenagoras, implying, as the latter does not, that we offer our prayers and thanks neither in a theological vacuum nor in a purely creation-orientated context. Rather, we 'sacrifice' not only as creatures, but as redeemed creatures. Here, perhaps, are the very faint beginnings of the sense that we have no offering independently of Christ's death; but we do not have as yet any sense that there is a kind of rivalry between Calvary as sacrifice and the eucharist as sacrifice. This is largely because most of the Christian writers of this period shared the general distaste for the language of propitiation—and did not, in any case, assume that all sacrifice was propitiatory.[2] It is still quite possible to work within a wide and loose nexus of sacrificial ideas without raising the question of the 'full, final, sacrifice'; indeed it would be hard to defend Christianity as a legitimate phenomenon without being prepared to talk like this. It is assumed, of course, that Christ has abolished the ceremonial law of the Old Covenant (this is the burden of much of Justin's *Dialogue),* but this does not mean a radical discontinuity between the church and 'religion', Jewish or pagan. However, it seems to be felt necessary to avoid simply collapsing Christian life and liturgy into 'natural religion', prayer and good deeds: hence the importance of a visible ritual 'sacrifice' explicitly anchored in the history of Christ as the vehicle of sacrificial prayer. We are, as Christians, priests; but we[3] are not so by natural right. It is

---

[1] *Dialogue* 117—an obscure passage, but the meaning is probably as I have summarized it. *Kai ep 'anamnesei . . .* must mean, 'And Christians so do [sc. give thanks to God] in the remembrance made by means of food and drink . . .'.

[2] It is one of the great strengths of Dr. Young's monograph that this is made abundantly plain. Pp.185-192 suggest that only in the post-Nicene period (*in* Greek Christian literature at least) does the association of Calvary with propitiation become at all significant. How important is it that this coincides with a dramatic decline in actual sacrificial practice as a social reality? Is there more freedom to use the language when it is more clearly *not* anchored in the literal shedding of sacrificial blood as a regularly visible phenomenon?

[3] Justin, *Dialogue* 116.

by grace that we are given a sacrifice (Justin's repeated expression[1]) and accounted worthy to 'stand and serve as priests' in the presence of God.[2]

The eucharist says something, then, about the priestly character of the church and, obliquely, something about its relation to the world and the world's welfare. Mention of it as sacrificial serves the apologetic purpose of legitimizing Christianity as non-magical, non-atheistic, as concerned with the harmony and continuity of things—with tradition, rite, and custom, and with political obligation. But there is an incipient eucharistic theology behind this slightly *ad hoc* set of arguments. We have seen Justin beginning to spell this out; but it is Irenaeus who deals with it most fully. His fundamental conviction, stated in *Adversus Haereses* IV.14, is that God is characterized in all he does by utterly gratuitous generosity *(munificentia)*—i.e. he needs nothing, because in himself he has the fulness of praise and glory: Word and Father give glory to each other eternally. What God asks of us is thus for our good, not his. In 15, he goes on to interpret the Mosaic Law in this light, and in 17 turns to the question of sacrifice. To see sacrifice as propitiatory is to fall into the trap of supposing that God needs things from us: like all ordinances, sacrifice is meant to keep God's people from idolatry and to guarantee their grateful remembrance of him. But it will only be itself, therefore, in the context of that comprehensive justice and compassion which is true mindfulness of God.

All sacrifice is thus expressive rather than functional; and the same is true of the offering commanded by Christ. Christians are given an offering to make, so that they may not be 'unfruitful or ungrateful' (17.5): as with Justin, we are constituted a sacrificing priesthood because of Christ's gift. But what exactly is this gift? We are enjoined to offer the *primitiae*, 'first-fruits', of creation (the original Greek was presumably, as Rousseau has it, *aparchas*[3]). and subsequently reminded that we are nourished by the *primitiae* of his gifts in the new covenant'. Now an offering of bread and wine is not a 'first-fruits' offering in any obvious sense; we are not dealing with a Christian harvest festival. If we read Ireneus carefully, it seems that what he is saying is that Christ at the Last Supper took an offering from the creation, and by designating it as his body and blood constituted it a 'first fruits' of the *new* creation—*novi Testamenti novam . . . oblationem.*[4] Further, a little later on (17.6), Irenaeus implies that our sacrifice is pure

[1] *Ibid.* 40 and 117

[2] The well-known phrase is from 'Hippolytus' 's liturgy IV.11: see most conveniently G. Dix's version, *The Apostolic Tradition of St. Hippolytus of Rome* (London, 1937) p.9, and G. J. Cuming (ed.) *Hippolytus: A Text for Students* (Grove Liturgical Study no. 8, Grove Books, 1976).

[3] *Irénée de Lyon, Contre les Hérésies, IV,* ed. Adelin Rousseau (*Sources Chrétiennes* no. 100, Paris, 1965) p.591.

[4] The offering of first-fruits in Jewish practice followed closely on the Passover season, and the Feast of Weeks during which first-fruits were offered was associated in various ways with the covenant and its renewal. *Jubilees (VI and XV)* connects it with the Noachic and Abrahamic covenants; later Judaism (from the second century?) connected it with the giving of the Law. Irenaeus, as an Asian with Quartodeciman sympathies, *may* have known a little about the ramifications of Jewish festal lore: in which case the first-fruits/new covenant link here may not be fortuitous, and it is possible that a connection is being made between Christ's words about the new covenant in his blood and the first-fruits offering as a covenant renewal ceremony. But this must remain a speculation.

(Malachi again) because offered through Jesus Christ; and this is paralleled in 18.4, when we are told that the Jews can make no pure offering 'because they have not accepted the Word through whom it [the pure sacrifice] is offered to God.'[1] So the offering of created bread and wine through Christ becomes a fusion of earthly and heavenly realities (18.5), transformed by its association with Christ's command into a sign and anticipation of the new creation perfectly present in his person.

The association of the eucharist with Christ's death is not made—perhaps not surprisingly, given Irenaeus' general lack of interest in the imagery of propitiation by bloodshed (there are some isolated passages in the Latin which appear to speak in these terms, but their status and meaning is unclear). Harvey is right in his note on Irenaeus' eucharistic teaching[2] to say that if the eucharist is a sacrifice for Irenaeus it is a thank-offering, not a sin-offering. The 'paschal' aspect of the sacrament is muted, and the notion of a covenant in Christ's blood is in no way developed.[3] However, without any explicit statement that Christ is offered in the eucharist[4], Irenaeus has in fact moved a very considerable way towards some such position. Once again, there is no sense that eucharist and Calvary are in competition; but if we are a priestly people, sacramentally enacting our obedience and gratitude to God, bearing fruit for him, what we ritually offer is the beginning of the new creation's harvest—the humanity of Christ, in which the deification of human nature is perfected and offered to us (hence the eucharist's transforming properties—18.5). There are no clear distinctions between the offering (by us) of bread and wine, the offering (by us in Christ) of his deified humanity, and the offering (to us by Christ) of risen life through the 'nourishment' of the first fruits of new creation. We praise God worthily by 'presenting' Christ to him—both in our Christlike obedience and love and in our ritual offering. We glorify the name of God by glorifying the name of Jesus in our liturgy[5] (thus once more fulfilling Malachi's prophecy about incense being offered to the *name* of God)—a notion which refers us back to Irenaeus' starting point, that God and his Son eternally give glory to each other, sharing with one another the abundance of life and joy which is their nature. Our privilege is to reflect what Father and Son do: in the gratuity, the overflow of a thanksgiving which God does not need, we experience in ourselves something of God's own gratuity which is the giving of glory.

1 Reading *per quod offertur* rather than *quod offertur*. The earliest ms. supports the latter reading, but learned opinion tends to regard the former as *difficilior* and the latter as not really consonant with the rest of Irenaeus' treatment of the subject.

2 *Sancti Irenaei . . . adversus Haereses*, ed. W. W. Harvey (Cambridge, 1857) vol. II, p.209, n.2.

3 18.3 alludes vaguely to the suffering of the righteous as part of their 'sacrificial' obedience, but no connection is made with Christ's death.

4 Assuming the usual reading of 18.4 (cf. n.3, supra).

5 17.6. There are strong liturgical resonances here: both the *Didache* and the Liturgy of Addai and Mari show a very Semitic interest in the 'glorifying of the Name', and Irenaeus is very probably alluding to some familiar liturgical formula of this kind. On the background of these ideas, see especially Louis Bouyer, *Eucharist* (London and Notre Dame, 1968) pp.55-56, 97, etc., and J. Danielou, *The Theology of Jewish Christianity* (London, 1964) pp.147-163.

Hence Irenaeus' slightly unexpected introduction (18.6) of the image of the heavenly altar. Our prayers and offerings are directed heavenwards: we are told that in heaven there is a temple and a tabernacle (referring to Rev. 11.9 and 21.3), in which God and his human children dwell together. Praise at the heavenly altar is the union through the incarnate work of Christ, of our offering with the mutual glorifying of Father and Son: and this praise, this offering (as Irenaeus has made clear in the preceding section) is primarily our gratuitous love for the poor and deprived—free love as gratitude, of which the ritual offering is the articulation.

Professor Hanson sums up 'Irenaeus' doctrine of eucharistic offering' thus:

> 'he teaches that Christians offer to God bread and wine so that at their prayer he may make them into the body and blood of Christ in order to enable the Christians to communicate'.[1]

This seems to me rather bald, as does Fr. Daly's comment:

> 'All the evidence suggests that the eucharistic sacrifice is, as it was for Justin, the spiritualized one of prayers of praise and thanksgiving.'[2]

Irenaeus' nexus of images is far richer than either of these epitomes suggests. Once we grasp his fundamental principle that sacrifice is only a 'necessity' as a natural ritual expression of grateful love, it is possible to see taking shape a link between the earthly offering of praise and the eternal 'liturgy' of the Trinity—a point extensively developed in various ways in later liturgies. Of course, the ritual offering *adds* nothing to the work of Christ, and the connecting of the whole discussion to the prior reality of God's inner relatedness leaves no room for ambiguity about where the ultimate agency and initiative lies. We do not work our salvation in offering the eucharistic oblation; we witness to the share we have been given in the glorified life of Christ, manifest in the rest of our lives as charity, humility, and pity. And the purity of our offering depends upon our commitment to the Christ through whom it is offered.

This is to schematize Irenaeus unduly in some ways; but it is important to see that—as in so many other areas of theology—he lays a tantalizing trail of allusions and undeveloped resonances to await more systematic exploration. The gap in his presentation seems to be in reference to Christ's death: not for him the assumption that sacrifice is essentially to do with death. Even in those passages (see, e.g. *Adversus Haereses* 111.9) where he speaks of Christ's redeeming blood and reconciling passion, the language is largely Pauline, and he does little to make it his own. Fr. Daly[3] refers us to a passage in Irenaeus' *Demonstration of the Apostolic Preaching,* 31 in which there is mention of Christ's 'offering up' human nature in his person 'on behalf of his forefathers'; but nothing even here directly implies a view of Christ's *death* as uniquely sacrifical (as opposed to his humanity in general). Despite Irenaeus' heavy reliance on the rich Johannine language

[1] *Op. cit.* p.10.
[2] *Origins,* p.96.
[3] *Ibid.* p.93.

of the mutual giving-glory of Father and Son, the Fourth Evangelist's in-
sistence that it is the *cross* of Jesus which represents, in our history, the
focus, the heart of this mutual glorifying is missing in the *Adversus
Haereses*.

Nonetheless, the perspectives opened up here are salutary. Once it is
clear that no Christian 'sacrifice' can be a bribe to God, because nothing
can add to his abundance, and his mercy never needs to be coerced, we
are free to consider the eucharist as a gift whose sole motive and purpose
is gratitude—a gift which therefore shares the character of the Son's
eternal praise of the Father in being an act of gratuitous love, and so may
be called an offering of the Son to the Father. We give what we have been
given—the flesh and blood of Jesus which opens to us the vision of
eternal praise and glorification. To see the eucharist in such terms prevents
us from falling into the obvious and dangerous traps of treating our prayer
and praise and thanksgiving as primarily functional, designed to obtain
something, or at least to fulfil an obligation whose non-fulfilment would
cause God to withdraw his grace; and of separating our worship from the
life of God, which as Christians we enter at baptism—i.e., of separating
our self-offering in life and prayer from that of Christ on which ours
always rests. A moment's reflection should make it plain that these two
dangers are closely connected; prayer as giving glory, ascribing 'worth' to
another, cannot be a means to any end except the confirmation and deepen-
ing of an existing relation of intimate trust.

3 THE ALTAR IN HEAVEN

Irenaeus speaks of a heavenly altar and temple, developing a long-standing convention in Jewish and Christian usage; but, although he uses Paul's language about the body as God's (and Christ's) temple, he does not seem to pick up the idea of the church itself as temple.[1] This, however, opens up a parallel and complementary pattern of ideas to the one we have already examined, a tradition of seeing Christ and the church as interchangeably altar, temple, and sacrifice. There are passages in the New Testament which suggest a model of the community as temple—1 Cor. 3.10-17, 1 Peter 2.4-8, possibly Heb. 3.6, and Rev. 3.12 and 21, 14; others which suggest that the community (or at least its life and deeds) is a sacrifice—Rom. 12.1, Phil. 2.17, 4.18. God and the Lamb are together the temple of the New Jerusalem in Rev. 21.22, and Christ in the days of his flesh can be described as a temple in John 2.21. The 'altar from which those who serve the tent have no right to eat' in Heb. 13.10 is presumably Jesus; and it is possible that the *hilasterion* of Rom. 3.25 is to be identified with the mercy-seat in the Holy of Holies. In short, temple and cult language is not uncommon in the New Testament in the context of speaking about the Messiah and his community.

The Qumran texts have underlined the pre-Christian provenance of this kind of imagery.[2] A famous passage in the *Manual of Discipline*[3] speaks of the community not only as temple but as sacrifice[4]: the lay community, it appears, is the Holy Place, the priestly body is the Holy of Holies, and the atoning sacrifice is the whole life of the community in its observance of the Law and its sufferings for the sake of righteousness. The same text from Isaiah (28.16) is referred to here as is quoted in 1 Peter 2.6, and there can be no doubt that a common background must be assumed. However, nowhere in early Christian literature is there any indication that the *church* could be seen as an atoning sacrifice: the biblical passages which use sacrificial imagery of the church may imply no more than the incense-offering as a prototype, an offering which is simply an aspect of the regular temple observance of thanksgiving and commemoration.[5]

[1] *Ibid.* pp.94-95; the exception alleged on p.95 n.8 in *Adversus Haereses* IV. 17 (§ IV. 8, in the numeration employed above, following Rousseau) seems to me an entirely inconclusive case.

[2] For a full discussion, see Bertil Gartner, *The Temple and Community in Qumran and the New Testament* (Cambridge, 1965).

[3] 105 *VIII-IX*, For text, translation and notes, see P. Wernberg-Möller, *The Manual of Discipline* (Leiden, 1957) esp. pp.124f.

[4] *VIII* 10-11: *vehayu le rason le khapper b'ad ha-ares.*

[5] The solemn incense-offering on the 'altar of gold' within the Holy Place is a part of the daily *(tamid)* sacrificial rites of the temple in the P traditions of the Pentateuch, and so has a sacrificial import (see M. Haran, *Temples and Temple-Service in Ancient Israel* (Oxford, 1978) pp.241-245); but as a *tamid* ritual, it is separate from the complex of sin—and purification—offerings. In apocalyptic, there is *only* an incense-altar in the heavenly sanctuary, as there can be no animal sacrifice in heaven (see R. H. Charles, *The Revelation of St. John* (Edinburgh, 1920) vol. 1, p.227-228). This is a point of some significance: if there is no animal sacrifice (the sacrifice of irrational creatures), the heavenly offering is a *rational (logike)* one: so it is described in the *Testament of Levi (III.6)*. This is evidently the vocabulary underlying Rom. 12.1, etc.—Christians offer what the angels offer, 'the pleasing savour of a rational and bloodless sacrifice'.

It may indeed be that one of the aims of the writer to the Hebrews is not only to direct a polemic against orthodox temple cultus but also to insist that the atoning offering, while it is an offering of total obedience and the consequent martyrdom, *can only* be made by one whose priesthood is intrinsic to his very being, who makes atonement not for himself but for his people, whose obedience is total—only by God's unique Son, not by any 'new temple' community.

If Christ as high priest has an atoning sacrifice *(le rason le khapper* in the Qumran phrase), it is himself, the achievement of his obedience and the blood of his martyrdom; but as priest he offers not only an atonement sacrifice but a thank-offering, a sacrifice of praise (Heb. 13.15). 'He offers'—in the sense that we are only able to offer thanks and praise through him, because of what he has done; our praise and thanksgiving is the incense he offers perpetually in the heavenly shrine. This is, I think, a defensible unpacking of Heb. 13, especially in the light of the widespread image in Jewish apocalyptic of the heavenly intercessor offering the prayers— and sometimes the souls—of the righteous, an image echoed in 8.3.[1] Thus, if the church is conceived as itself a sacrifice, it is in this sense: its worship, its petition, and, probably, its self-sacrificial devotion (the souls of the martyrs) all constitute the heavenly *tamid,* offered by Jesus, the Great Angel or angel of peace, who is mediator and intercessor. In this context—as Charles and others have suggested—the exalted Christ takes on some of the characteristics of the archangel Michael.[2]

Some such complex of ideas must have been in the background of a good deal of Jewish Christian thinking in the first two centuries of our era. Because it is by its very nature oblique, allusive, and associative, it is difficult to express in ordered theological conceptuality; but I shall try to untangle it a little. Non-Christian Judaism, in the first century and earlier, was familiar with two interrelated ideas: that there is a heavenly intercessor who presents the prayers of the righeous as an incense-offering in the heavenly shrine; and that the souls of the martyrs (or, for the Qumran sect simply the radically obedient lives of the community) constitute an atoning sacrifice. The symbolism is obviously complicated when there is talk of the martyrs being 'offered' on the heavenly altar: they are a quasi-blood-sacrifice, yet there appears to be only one altar (for *animaktos,* 'bloodless', sacrifice) in heaven. The *Testament of Levi* (III.6) describes the bloodless offering in heaven as itself 'propitiation' (the angels are *leitourgountes kai exilaskomenoi),* but nothing here suggests any parallel with the Levitical atonement rites.

Whether consciously or not, early Christianity (Paul, Hebrews, Revelation, in the first instance) reorganized this symbolism into a more intelligible form. There is only one atoning or 'propitiating' sacrifice leaving aside for now the exact sense of the *hilaskesthai* cluster of words), and it is

---

1 Charles, *op. cit.,* I, pp.225-226, 230; Cf. 183-174.
2 In addition to Charles *(The Testaments of the Twelve Patriarchs,* London, 1980, pp.33-34, n.5, 132, n.2; with these passages from the Testaments, Cf. I Enoch IX, *passim, XV.2, LXXXIX.* 76), see Daniélou *op. cip.,* pp.123-127 (though this has relatively little to say about the specifically *priestly* role of Michael in the heavenly liturgy—perhaps because the most explicit texts about this are in much later Jewish sources).

Christ's death, effected on earth, in flesh, 'received' in heaven; but what that heavenly acceptance of the offering means is that Christian prayer and life are present before God, at his heavenly altar and throne.[1] Thus the death of the *Christian* martyr cannot be a propitiation, but it can be an 'acceptable offering', presented by Christ in heaven. It is therefore intelligible to talk about the church on earth as a fundamentally sacrificial phenomenon: it is a place where offering is made, and there is nothing surprising in its being described as a shrine or an altar, or its members as priests—though it is a shrine because it manifests the heavenly altar, the underlying reality of Christ's intercession, and Christians are priests entirely in a derivative sense: they 'offer', which is the characteristic priestly act, but only because they are *being offered* by the eternal high priest, and because they have been made a worthy offering by the atonement achieved *ephapax* in the cross.

So far from the sacrifice of Calvary excluding the possibility of any other sacrifice, it is the cross and its 'reception' as an offering by the Father in the glorification of the crucified Son which constitutes those who are won through the cross a priestly people, a 'temple community'. Like the Qumran sectaries, they are both shrine and sacrifice; but unlike them they are not so in virtue of their own faithfulness, but because of the faithfulness *usque ad mortem* of the sole authentic priest, the one who cannot be anything other than priest, whose priestly life and death constitute the ground of all subsequent offering. And if we are looking for an analogy to this in the Judaism of the day, we do in fact possess a parallel in the *Aqedah* tradition, the cluster of legend and imagery centred on the Binding of Isaac.[2] A ram or, rather, a male lamb in rabbinic tradition, specially created, is provided as a sacrifice to redeem Isaac, in return for his willingness to be sacrificed himself, and this is the point at which the *tamid* offering is instituted, the sacrifice of a lamb morning and evening in the temple. When the lambs are offered, God 'sees' and remembers the *Aqedah*[3], which is itself an offering for sin in some sense—so that the memorial of the *Aqedah* constitutes a plea for mercy and grace, even though it is not as such a sin-offering.[4] Since early Jewish tradition (pre-second century

[1] On the close association of throne and altar in apocalyptic, see Charles, *Revelation*, I, pp.112, 228-229, 231.

[2] Full discussions in R. Le Deaut *La Nuit Pascale* (Rome, 1963); G. Vermes, 'Redemption and Genesis xxii', in *Scripture and Tradition in Judaism* (Leiden, 1961, 2nd ed. 1973); R. Hayward's appendix to S. W. Sykes 'Sacrifice in the New Testament and Christian Theology', in M.F.C. Bourdillon and M. Fortes (ed.) *Sacrifice* (London and New York, 1980).

[3] See, e.g., *Lev. Rabbah II.*11: 'The Sages said: When Abraham, our father, bound Isaac his son, the Holy One, blessed be He, instituted the sacrifice of two he-lambs, one in the morning and one in the evening. Why did He do this?—When Israel offer up the daily sacrifices on tha altar, and read this verse, viz. *"Zafonah before the Lord"*, the Holy One, blessed be He, remembers the binding of Isaac' (tr. from *The Midrash*, ed. H. Freedman and M. Simon, vol. IV (London, 1939) p.31). *Safonah* in Lev. 1.11, meaning 'on the north side of the altar', is taken to be connected with *safah,* 'to see': thus *'safonah* before the Lord' equals 'before the Lord, so that he may see [sc. the binding of Isaac]'. This is presumably a Palestinian tradition, like the majority of midrash interpretations, and there is no reason for supposing it to be later than the first century A.D.

[4] *Gen Rabbah LVI.* 9 and 10.

A.D.) connected the *Aqedah* to the Passover season, along with creation, the Abrahamic covenant, the birth of Isaac, and the hope of the Messiah's coming[1], it is clear that the ransoming of Isaac by the provision of a lamb was seen as one of God's decisive acts of honouring his promises—a kind of renewal of the covenant built into creation[2], expressed in the promise to Abraham, vindicated at the Exodus, consummated in the Messianic age.[3]

Thus both the *tamid* sacrifice and the Passover celebration are 'memorials' of a foundational event without which subsequent offerings would not occur and would not be effective. The *Aqedah* institutes a sacrificial tradition, a ritual of offering which has no independent force, but whose goal and function is to petition God to be faithful to the covenant he has already honoured by ransoming Isaac; the Passover proclaims, with another kind of memorial sacrifice, God's fidelity to what he has done. Behind both in this tradition is the mythological picture of a prior act of God in creation to provide for a ransoming sacrifice—the foreordained lamb. And both *Aqedah* and Passover-Exodus traditions speak in their various ways, of an act constituting Israel a priestly, a sacrificing, people.

The degree to which *Aqedah* traditions are present in the New Testament is much debated. If Jesus really did speak about a new covenant in his blood at a Passover meal, and if the Passover-*Aqedah* link were already vivid in the minds of Jews of that time, it would be hard to avoid the conclusion that the eucharistic rite was meant to be to the cross as the *tamid* offering was to the *Aqedah*[4]; and even if this association of cup and covenant does not go back to Jesus himself, it was rapidly made in the early communities. What is more, as Vermes has indicated[5], Jeremias' familiar point that we should take Jesus' alleged words, 'Do this for my memorial' (1 Cor. 11.24-25, Luke 22.19) as meaning, 'Do this so that God may remember me'[6] would make far better sense in relation to the *Aqedah*. God is besought to show himself once again the God he has shown himself to be in giving Jesus as a ransom for the children of promise: the 'sacrifice' of bread and cup is in no way an expiation or propitiation of sin, but a prayer that we may see and grasp God as he is, a God who mercifully sends a sacrificial redeemer to us: a God whose property it is to provide himself a lamb for sacrifice.

So we are led back again to the idea of the eucharist as a celebration of God's *gratuitous* love. We cannot effect anything new through our offering,

1 Jubilees and the Palestinian Targum both bear out the Passover link.
2 The lamb of the *Aqedah* was held to be created on the first sabbath eve. Vermes, Hayward, and others, point to the probable allusion to this in 1 Peter 1.19-20 and Rev. 13.8.
3 It is worth noting that there is a *hekhalot* poem on the *Aqedah*, probably from the period of Byzantine rule in Palestine, which explicitly asks God to 'reckon to us the covenant' made with Isaac by the provision of the sacrificial lamb *(Tizkor—lanu beritho, tinsor-lanu 'aqedatho:* lit. 'be mindful for us of his covenant, preserve for us [? in your memory] his binding'). For text and a slightly different translation, see T. Carmi *The Penguin Book of Hebrew Verse* (London, 1981) p.102.
4 This is Vermes' conclusion *(op. cit.,* pp.225-227), though he does not draw out the point about covenant-renewal as part of the memorial of the *Aqedah*.
5 *Ibid.* p.226.
6 J. Jeremias *The Eucharistic Words of Jesus* (S.C.M., London, 1966) pp.237-255.

because God has acted first, acted according to his nature: he has determined to be the ground of our beseeching by giving us the means to draw near to him, inviting us to make covenant with him, sealing the covenant by showing his will to rescue and accept and forgive. In the death of Jesus, God builds a temple and ordains a priesthood because Jesus' death in the light of his exaltation speaks of an unparalleled closeness to God: i.e. his death constitutes a 'consecration', a drawing near to 'the holy' in its deepest reality; and, by contact with the event, his followers may be made holy (John 17.11-19). Jesus in his death defines a 'holy space', a place of reconciliation between sacred and profane orders. a place too of unlimited accessibility, unlike the veiled shrine of the old temple (hence the legend of the tearing of the veil in Matt. 27.51). Those who through his sacrifice are brought near to the holy, to the source of judgment, creativity and significance, to the Father, are themselves made holy: and so one can say almost indifferently that they *are* the temple, that they are *in* the temple, that they offer sacrifice or that they are an offering. Whatever the image, they are a 'holy space' where praise of God's generosity, the acknowledgment of an order of being utterly beyond need, achievement, demand, can be enacted: an image of 'heaven', a manifestation of the nature of the angelic liturgy.[1] Yet this acknowledgment is made, this praise is offered, because of the manifesting to us of gratuitous love in Jesus' death and resurrection. *That* is his consecration, as it is ours: that is what makes us a priestly people, offering the incense of our love and praise, and the memorial of the new covenant.

[1] It is important that one of our earliest liturgical survivals, Addai and Mari, so stresses the priority of the angelic praise which we, though 'lowly, weak and miserable', are privileged to share.

4. CHURCH AND ALTAR IN IGNATIUS

In case this sounds simply like a piece of rather fanciful exegesis, resting upon what are confessedly disputed points of interpretation and cross-reference, I shall turn for illustration to a writer whose sacrificial and cultic imagery is still rather under-explored—Ignatius of Antioch.[1] We find in his writings precisely that curious mélange of imagery I have outlined, and, assuming that not all of it is wholly peculiar to him, his language reinforces the idea that early Christianity, certainly in the Semitic world at least, was quite heavily preoccupied with the idea of the church as a sacrificial reality.

It is no surprise to find in *Ephes.9* the Pauline and Petrine image of the faithful as stones of the temple; but later in the same chapter, Ignatius shifts his metaphor to that of a religious procession in which believers are *theophoroi, naophoroi, Christophoroi*—bearers of God, bearers of the shrine, bearers of Christ. The image may well depend upon the practice of pagan religious processions in which idols were carried in small shrines; but there may also be a—rather fugitive—reference to the portable tabernacle of the Pentateuch.[2] Rather clearer is the passage in *Magn.* 7, exhorting the church to gather to the one *naos,* God, and the one *thusiasterion,* Christ. Here Christ is evidently associated with the altar (probably the altar of incense)—presumably as the one who presents the faithful and their prayers to God, identified with the Holy of Holies and its mercy-seat. This is borne out by *Ephes.* 5: being 'within the altar' is, at the most obvious level, being in the inner court of the temple or even in the Holy Place (depending which altar is meant)[3]; but the implication, here and elsewhere (in *Trall.* 7, for instance), is that being in or within or within reach of the altar is being united with Christ, the altar on which the sacrifice of our prayer is offered. Given all that has been said about the importance of the incense-altar in apocalyptic, it seems more likely that the phrase does not in fact designate the court of the altar of burnt-offering. According to *Trall.* 7, which uses the identical phrase, to be 'within the altar' is to be 'pure', and to be 'inseparable' from Christ (and the bishop): acting independently of the church assembled around the bishop is cutting onself off from the altar, i.e. from the mediation and intercession of Christ.

But where *is* the church visibly assembled around the bishop? At the eucharist. *Philad.* 4 emphasizes the one eucharist as an absolute priority,

---

1 Professor Hanson barely mentions Ignatius in his study *(op. cit.,* pp.86-87). Henning Paulsen's *Studien zur Theologie des Ignatius von Antiochien* (Göttingen, 1978) has some desultory remarks on pp.146, 156-157.

2 Or the ark; but this is most unlikely. *Naos,* though just possible for the Holy of Holies, is not used in Septuagintal or patristic Greek for the ark.

3 Lightfoot takes the phrase to refer to the 'court of the congregation', i.e., he assumes that the altar is the altar of burnt-offering. (See Lightfoot, *The Apostolic Fathers,* vol. II, (2nd edn.) London 1889, pp.43-44).. Mt 23.35 would support this interpretation, but it is not all that easy to imagine an identification of Christ with the altar of burnt-offering. However, it would be a mistake to look for absolute clarity and consistency in this kind of symbolism.

'for *one* is the flesh of our Lord Jesus Christ, *one* is the cup we drink for unity through his blood; one altar we have, as we have one bishop.' There is no need to take 'altar' here as meaning the eucharistic table itself to grasp that the eucharist is seen as a participation in Christ's offering— a drawing near to the altar upon which he, as a consequence of his sacrificial death, presents us to his Father as those 'involved in' or 'associated with' his passion *(Philad.* 3: *'to(i) pathei . . . sygkatatithetai').*[1] The sign of cutting oneself off from Christ is separation from the bishop's liturgical meeting—most importantly (so *Philad.* 4 suggests) the eucharistic gathering, but also *(Smyrn.* 8) the baptismal rite. To be visibly, significantly, associated with Christ's ransoming death and its fruits is to be at the bishop's eucharist: this is what it means in practice to be 'within the altar'. Or, to put it a little differently, the church's priestly-sacrificial nature, in virtue of its being brought to the sanctuary by Christ the high priest *(Philad.* 9—to Christ is 'committed' the holy of holies, he is the door through which the saints of old and new covenants enter the Father's presence), is manifested in the unity of the eucharist, where believers are brought together in sharing the sacrificed flesh and blood of Jesus *(Smyrn.* 6). The eucharist is the culminating expression of God's gift, and to refuse the eucharist is to refuse the love of God and the love of humanity, to be incapable of receiving *(ibid.* 6-7). And, if *Rom.* 7 refers even indirectly to the eucharist, the emphasis is again on gift—the bread of God which comes down from heaven (cf. *Ephes.* 5), the blood of Christ which is never-failing love.

What is prior is the gift of God: he has given us not only a high priest through whose eternal intercession or mediation all the righteous are presented before the mercy-seat, but a perfecting of this continuing process through the earthly life and death and resurrection of the high priest himself *(Philad.* 9)—presumably because through the incarnation we are not only presented by the high priest, but in sort united with him, sharing his 'incorruptible' life. And since the eucharist is described as 'the medicine which brings immortality' *(Ephes.* 20), it is clearly above all else a share in the gift which is Jesus' incarnate self-ascrifice.

Ignatius himself evidently thought of his death as a sacrifice *(Rom.* 2.4), even a sacrifice on behalf of the churches *(Ephes.* 21, *Smyrn.* 10, *Pol.* 2, in all of which occurs the word *antipsychon.* which normally means a vicarious sacrifice).[2] The passage in *Rom.* 4 which speaks of the martyr being ground into 'pure bread' by the teeth of the wild beasts suggests an analogy with the offering of pure loaves at Pentecost[3]—i.e., not with a blood-sacrifice or atoning sacrifice; and although other passages go a good deal further, it is doubtful whether Ignatius meant the language of vicarious death to be taken in an absolutely strict sense. Even allowing that there is an important dimension of 'vicarious' imagery in this, if we read these passages in the light of *Romans* as a whole it is plain that the

---

[1] Paulsen *(op. cit.* p.156) attempts to deny that *thusiasterion* here has any sacrificial sense; given the references to 'passion' and 'blood' in the context, this is an extraordinary judgment.

[2] See Lightfoot's admirable note, *Apostolic Fathers* II, pp.87-88.

[3] *Ibid.*, p.207.

consummation of the martyr's sacrifice is precisely the perfection in the martyr of the prior image of the sacrificed Christ, 'in' or 'by' the Holy Spirit *(Rom.* 8). These phrases should not, therefore, be taken to qualify the general sense in Ignatius' letters of the dependence of Christian offering—self-offering and ritual offering—upon the sacrifice of Christ.

The point of all this is to show how an early Semitic Christian[1] can be strikingly free with a wide range of cultic images, evidently understanding the Christian church as a place of sacrifice, without any sign of feeling that there is a problem as to whether we have one sacrifice or several. There is no reason to think that he had any familiarity with the *Aqedah* traditions (his background is not Rabbinic or Palestinian), but there is a structural parallel, possibly mediated through Paul, Hebrews, even 1 Peter, in the notion of a 'foundational' sacrifice offered by God for human beings (or *a* human being) to offer, establishing a cultic pattern, in which all other offerings depend on this prior act, and are to some extent therefore memorial and thanksgiving sacrifices, rather than having independent efficacy.[2]

---

[1] Quite probably of Gentile background, but (a) relatively unacquainted with systematic philosophical concepts and thus more inclined to 'think in symbols,' and (b) familiar with the Old Testament—and possibly with the Letter to the Hebrews—and thus familiar with Jewish cultic language and perhaps with Christian modifications of it.

[2] There is, incidentally, a further obvious structural parallel in the Vedic Hindu myth of creation as the self-sacrifice of a primal 'person.' which establishes sacrifice as the axis of all future religious observance. See the brilliant synthesis of Ananda Coomaraswamy, 'Atmayajna: Self-Sacrifice' in Vol. II of his collected works, *Collected Papers: Metaphysics,* ed. R. Lipsey (Princeton, 1977) pp.107-147.

5. OFFERING THE OFFERER: THE SYRIAN TRADITION

Nor is this an individual peculiarity of Ignatius. On the contrary, this particular view of sacrifice in the church—that it is, so to speak, a constant confession of dependence upon a single foundational event—is prominent in later Syrian theology, especially in the work of Ephrem. Ephrem is much preoccupied with the incarnational reversal of God's relation with his creatures: the source and sustains of all becomes dependent on what he sustains[1]—'the child I carry carries me, says Mary'.[2] A particularly powerful image for him is that of the priest Simeon 'offering' the child Jesus in the temple: and this becomes the occasion for some sustained reflection on what it means for the creature to 'offer' Christ. 'Blessed is that priest', writes Ephrem, 'who offered in the sanctuary the Father's Son to the Father'.[3] Simeon is given grace to carry the child, and his days are specially prolonged so that he may do so; and in his presenting of Christ, he is himself 'presented'.[4] The fullest development of the theme is in the long prose sermon *de Domino nostro,* where we read in §§ 50-53[5]:

> 'But Simeon the priest when he had received Christ in his arms so that he might present [offer] him to God, understood when he beheld him that he was not offering Christ but was himself being offered. For the Son is not to be offered to his Father by a servant; rather the servant is offered to his Lord by the Son. It is impossible that the one through whom every oblation [*qurban*] is offered would himself be offered by anyone else. The oblation does not offer the one who offers it but is offered by the offerer to God. And so the one who receives offerings gave himself to be offered by another, so that those who offered him might themselves be offered. Just as he gave his body to be eaten so that he might give life to the eaters while he was being eaten, so he surrendered himself to be an offering so as to sanctify by his cross the hands of those who offered him . . .
>
> (51) And so the Son came to the servant, not so that the Son might be offered by the servant, but so that the servant should, through the Son, offer to his Lord the ministry of priesthood and prophecy entrusted to him. Prophecy and priesthood, given by Moses were handed down to Simeon . . . Therefore Simeon offered up the Lord, and the two gifts became his . . . While Simeon made his offering before the Lord . . . he poured out upon him these two gifts, priesthood with his hands, prophecy with his lips.'

[1] Among numerous examples, see Hymn XXII *de nativitate (Corpus Scriptorum Christianonum Orientalium.* 186/187, *Scriptores Syri* 82/83, ed. Dom Edmund Beck (Louvain, 1959) pp.117-120 in the Syriac, 106-109 in Beck's German Translation); also Hymns IV and XVIII *de nativitate* (ibid., Syriac pp.25-45, esp. pp.38-40, German pp.24-38, esp. pp.34-35; and Syriac p.87, German p.79).

[2] The opening of Hymn XVII *de nativitate.*

[3] Hymn XXV *de nativitate (ibid.,* Syriac p.132, German p.119). The verb to 'offer' here is *qareb,* which becomes increasingly in later Syrian liturgies (e.g. the anaphorae of 'Nestorius' and 'Theodore of Mopsuestia') a specific term for the oblation of the eucharistic elements as opposed to the offering of thanks and praise (I am most grateful to the Rev. Bryan Spinks for information on this point).

[4] Hymn IV *de nativitate (ibid.,* Syriac p.44, German p.38); the verb is again *qareb.*

[5] CSCO 270/271, SS 116/117, ed. Dom Edmund Beck (Louvain, 1966) pp.47-50 in the Syriac, 48-51 in the German. For Christ offering us in the eucharist, there is a close parallel in Luther; see Bryan Spinks *Luther's Liturgical Criteria and His Reform of the Canon of the Mass* (Grove Liturgical Study no. 30, Grove Books, 1982) p.29.

This densely-packed text makes clear not only the eucharistic 'resonance' of the story of Christ's presentation in the temple but the connection between the eucharistic oblation and the cross. In the presentation, in the eucharist, and in the crucifixion, the agency appears to be human; but in fact all that human beings are doing in each of these instances is involving themselves in the divine action which presents them to the Father. What the human act of offering does is to 'give' Christ the exercise of priesthood in the world, i.e. to render his humanity a priestly (and prophetic) reality. Simeon ordains Christ priest, designates his incarnate form as charged with a priestly mission; and when the Son comes now to his servants to 'be offered', they (in confessing their dependence on him) yield their priesthood to him, and are offered to the Father at his hands.

So elsewhere in Ephrem: Christ is the 'chief of all sacrificers'[1], he is not sacrificed (on the cross) but sacrifices himself.[2] Instead of the sacrifices once offered in Jerusalem, one living victim is offered throughout all the world (which is now God's dwelling-place as Jerusalem was once believed to be), the self-sacrificed Lamb of God.[3] Christ alone is capable of being 'altar and lamb, victim and sacrificer, priest and [communion] meal'.[4] He offers sacrifice to himself, and breaks bread beforehand 'in a mystery' (b'raz) representing the sacrifice of Calvary.[5] So the last supper is a sacramental prefiguring of Calvary, and, when re-enacted as eucharist, it is again an act of Christ showing b'raz his saving death.

The way in which our eucharistic worship is united with Christ's offering is, characteristically, through the agency of the Holy Spirit. This is most vividly expressed in a well-known passage in Ephrem's Hymn X On Faith:
'Fire descended and consumed Elijah's sacrifices;
the Fire of mercies has become a living sacrifice for us.
Fire consumed the oblation;
we, Lord, have consumed your Fire in your oblation.'[6]

A great deal of this hymn employs similar imagery. The fire of the Spirit makes our oblation the life-giving gift of God, his oblation; as we have

---

[1] Hymn II de azymis (CSCO 248/249, SS 108-109, ed. Beck, Syriac p.4, German p.4) —the phrase is stronger than simply 'high priest', as Lamy's 1882 Latin version (princeps sacrificatorum) suggests.

[2] Ibid.

[3] Hymn XXI de azymis (ibid., Syriac p.41, German p.33).

[4] Hymn III de crucifixione (ibid., Syriac p.52, German p.41). Note the passage a little later (12) in which we read that the 'bread of the presence' (the shewbread) was broken on the cross—a further 'sanctuary' allusion—and that the cross was both the first altar and the first church, because the 'first of sacrifices' was performed upon it.

[5] Hymn II de azymis (ibid.).

[6] CSCO 154/155, SS 73/74, ed. Beck, Louvain, 1955, Syriac p.51, German p.35. Translation by Sebastian Brock, in a fine introductory essay on Ephrem, 'The Poet as Theologian' (Sobornost, Series 7, no. 4, 1977, pp.243-250), p.249. Another translation (with commentary) of the entire hymn, by Robert Murray, S. J., can be found in 'A Hymn of St. Ephrem to Christ on the Incarnation, the Holy Spirit and the Sacraments' in Eastern Churches Review, 3, 1970, pp.142-150. 'Sacrifice' and 'offering' here are once more qurban,

received the Spirit's 'fire' in baptism, so our offering is kindled by the same fire. A great deal has been written about the enormous significance of the Spirit in Syrian sacramental theology[1], and it is clear that for Ephrem and the tradition he represents there is a close connection between the Spirit's work in baptism and the possibility of our offering being offered by Christ. In the Syrian idea of Mary as type of the church, the crucial point is that Mary is filled with the Spirit so that she may bear the Christ who in fact (see above) 'bears' her.[2] The church as a whole is—in Aphrahat, for example[3]—the temple of the Spirit, the place where sin is taken away. The Spirit is given in baptism to purify the of our prayers, and part of the baptismal rite itself is the receiving of Christ's sacrificed body and blood.[4] The eucharist and baptism are both inseparably the receiving of Holy Spirit, constituting believers the dwelling place of the Spirit, a temple in which pure offering may be made. Our offering—in prayer generally and in the eucharist especially—'invites' the transforming action of the Holy Spirit, because it is offered by the baptized who are already kindled by the Spirit.

The idea that we are already, in baptism, united with the self-offering of Jesus is a central point in this complex of ideas. The sacraments are clearly grasped as belonging together, and baptism, the 'Easter' of every Christian, is seen as what makes the Church the shrine in which Christ exercises his priesthood in relation to us. Common baptism connects us to the one priest and his priestly act of consecrating and offering himself: we appear to take him to ourselves, but it is, more fundamentally, he who takes us to himself; and good Christian prayer—and liturgy—rests on an acknowledgment of that deeper reality, that undergirding action. It sees in the passion and resurrection the act in which God through Christ actively draws us to himself; in the words of 'Hippolytus', Christ fulfilled his Fathers' will and won for him a holy people, by stretching out his hands for voluntary suffering.[5] The effect of his offering, which we make our own in baptism, is to make us holy, priestly, capable of pure praise: we give to God because we have received from God.

---

[1] Sebastian Brock has illuminatingly discussed the consequent parallel between the eucharistic invocation of the Spirit and the Spirit's descent upon Mary at the Annunciation, a parallel developed in various Syriac liturgical commentaries. See his 'Mary and the Eucharist: an oriental perspective' in *Sobornost, incorporating the Eastern Churches Review,* vol. 1, no. 2, 1979, pp.50-59.

[2] Robert Murray's *Symbols of Church and Kingdom* (Cambridge, 1975) is the best general survey of these images.

[3] *Patrologia Syriaca* I, ed. R. Graffin (Paris, 1894) *Demonstratio XII de Paschate,* 8 (524-525).

[4] *Ibid. Demonstratio IV, de oratione,* 19 (181). §3 of this text, like Ephrem, uses the story of Elijah on Mount Carmel, but does not directly relate it to the Spirit in the eucharist.

[5] *Apostolic Tradition* IV. 7 (Dix, p.8).

6. SACRIFICE AND THE STRUCTURE OF THE LITURGY

In this light, it is of course rather unhelpful to search in primitive liturgies for 'moments' of offering or of consecration. Certainly it is artificial to schematize, as Dix does, the[1] 'two oblations', the church's and Christ's, and to suppose a clear distinction between the *anaphora* of the one and the *prosphora* of the other. Bouyer sees the development of formulae of oblation as an attempt to make explicit what is involved in 'memorializing' the cross; 'This oblation is nothing but the re-presentation to God of the pledge of salvation that he has given to his people in the "memorial". It acts as a basis for the prayer that the "mystery" of Christ, which is the soul of this memorial, may have its fulfilment in us. This comes down to our consecration as a people of priests, dedicated to the sole praise of the Father through the Son, in the power of the Spirit.[2] Thus the oblation-language serves as a bridge towards the invocation of the Spirit to consecrate and transform the gifts offered. But just as this consecratory climax is a relatively late development, so is the idea of a point at which the sacrifice of Christ is 'offered' in the eucharistic prayer.

Dr. Kenneth Stevenson has argued at some length[3] that the different 'families' of Eastern liturgies have quite widely differing views of what is offered in the eucharist and when. The Egyptian type appears to conceive the only offering involved as the placing of the elements upon the altar, whereas the Antiochene has generally an elaborate structure of commemoration and 'pleading' of Christ's sacrifice (the 'oblation') followed by a consecratory epiclesis—the whole of this being in various linguistic ways distinguished from the offering of worship. It might be added that the whole structure is further complicated by the tradition witnessed to in Theodore of Mopsuestia's Catecheses, which understands the offertory as in some sense sacrificial, and provides no simple means of distinguishing this from the sacrifice of the anaphora;[4] although some texts in this group make the distinction, the *ceremonial* focusing on the Great Entrance, and the ever-increasing para-liturgical elaboration connected with it, in the form of hymns concerned with Christ's death and burial, have left the Byzantine liturgy to this day a theologically rather disorderly composition. Dr. Stevenson's case may be questioned in a few points of detail, but the general conclusion stands: there is no one early Eastern pattern, no one clear eucharistic theology expressed in liturgical shape. There is no doubt that offering is taking place, but there may be several different expressions of it—as the oblation of bread and wine, or as the offering of these explicitly as a memorial of the passion, so that their offering constitutes a prayer for the fruits of Christ's offering, or as an offering of praise as a memorial. All agree that, in some way or other, *this* offering, the eucharistic rite, depends upon, reflects upon, and draws its fruitfulness from Calvary.

None of these forms shows any unease about offering as such, any sense of unworthiness to present gifts in the presence of God; more of this later.

---

1 Originally in Dix 'The Idea of "The Church" in the Primitive Liturgies' in A. G. Herbert (ed.) *The Parish Communign* (S.P.C.K., London, 1937) pp.95-143 (esp. pp.106-110, 111-115)—almost a highly-compressed draft of *The Shape of the Liturgy*.

2 *Eucharist*, p.183.

3 ' "Anaphoral Offering": Some Observations on Eastern Eucharistic Prayers' in *Ephemerides Liturgicae* 1980, pp.209-228.

4 See *ibid*. p.211.

But it is also true that none of them speaks of an active offering *by us* of Christ's body and blood. That would be possible only if the institution narrative were regarded as strictly consecratory—so that any 'offering' language afterwards would refer to the body and blood, and there really would be a 'sacrifice of Christ'. Dr. Tom Talley points out[1] that contemporary liturgical revisions in both the Anglican and the Roman Catholic churches have—inadvertently?—gone some considerable way towards such a view. The widespread reaction against an over-emphasized or over-dramatized offertory seems to have bred the idea that only consecration makes offering possible; only then do we have a suitable offering, Christ's body and blood. This has some ancestry in Catholic theology (though not, Talley stresses, in Thomas Aquinas), but remains theologically very ambiguous, and particularly uncongenial to the Reformed perspective outlined at the very beginning of this study. The body and blood made present—or evoked, or identified—in the eucharistic prayer do not represent an uncrucified (or unglorified) Jesus waiting to be offered; but if they do represent Jesus crucified and risen, the only possible form of our 'offering' them is by memorial. He is already present *as* sacrificed: his body and blood are saving, Spirit-filled realities, not dead passive objects.

We can refer back to Ephrem at this point. It seems that, in offering the signs of Jesus' flesh and blood, we offer him; but our job in worship is to yield the role of offerer to him, because he *has* offered—himself and his church. All this is far easier to bear in mind if we do not have a liturgical structure bound to dramatic 'changes of gear', suggesting that *here* we offer bread and wine, *here* is effected the transformation of these offerings, *here* we offer them again in a fashion that is somehow more solemn or effective. The recovery of a sense of unity in the eucharistic action and the eucharistic prayer is of great significance: though there is still visible, certainly in new Anglican liturgies, a residual bondage to the idea of *a* shape, with several clearly delimited stages.[2] Dr. Stevenson[3] finds the East Syrian anaphorae practically without 'sequenc or development', and although this is not quite true of the later liturgies, *Addai and Mari* certainly has little of either. Shapelessness is not in itself, of course, a virtue; it can mean a lack of intelligible boundaries. The gleeful chaos of mediaeval Ethiopian anaphorae has its appeal, but it is not all that helpful a model for purposive and nourishing liturgical action. Briefly, a eucharistic prayer should clearly proclaim what it is—a thankful confession of our dependence on God's covenanted grace, known in his 'name', through Jesus, renewed and sealed in the whole paschal event, betrayal, dereliction, death, and vindication. In this confession, our self-offering and our ritual offering are 'located' in the holy place of Christ's cross, where reconciliation is effected; and our gifts accepted on the heavenly altar, made into effective signs of God's 'bleeding love and mercy' (in Charles Wesley's phrase), are given to us again 'for the forgiveness of sins and a great hope of resurrection'.[4] Do we need much more 'sequence or development' than this?

[1] In an excellent essay on 'The Eucharistic Prayer: Tradition and Development', in Kenneth Stevenson (ed.) *The Liturgy Reshaped* (S.P.C.K., London, 1982).

[2] Rubric no. 36 in Rite A, suggests that 'taking' is part of an immutable structure.

[3] ' "Anaphoral Offering" ', p.227.

[4] *Addai and Mari*, §H, in Bryan Spinks' edition *Addai and Mari: A Text for Students* (Grove Liturgical Study no. 24, Grove Books, 1980) p.22.

7. SACRIFICE AND JUSTIFICATION

What, then, of the point briefly touched upon earlier, that we are unworthy to offer *any* sacrifice? This is a perfectly fair point as far as the notion of *atoning* sacrifice is concerned; but part of the assumption of this study is that, in Old and New Testament alike, the concept of sacrifice is a fluid one. Not until an exaggerated mediaeval passion-mysticism had pressed the identity of mass and Calvary to its extreme point, so that any 'sacrificing' in the eucharist *must* be the shedding of Christ's blood for the forgiveness of sins, does it appear that there might be a conflict here. Several of the Reformers—certainly Luther and Calvin—had no problem about the notions of memorial and thanksgiving sacrifice: Luther could understand the *Sanctus* as a praise,[1] Cranmer however, is more cautious. The third Exhortation and the Preface of the 1552 rite say a certain amount about thanksgiving for the history of salvation, but the rite is rather muted overall; and the idea of a *sacrifice* of thanksgiving is carefully transferred to the post-communion. The general emphasis prior to this is on penitence and pure need. It has been rather unkindly said that the only 'offering' in this liturgy before communion is of money—'the Alms for the Poor'.

This, I take it, is what Leslie Houlden meant by describing the evangelical Anglican understanding of the eucharist in terms of recapitulation of the conversion experience'.[2] Evangelicals[3] rightly protested that this was a most misleading phrase; but Houlden's point was that Cranmer's liturgy seems almost to assume that we are not 'in Christ' to begin with, that we have no right to approach the Father before we have received the pledges of Christ's sacrifice. This is not wholly fair to Cranmer, I realize, but it is clear that, although he distinguished theologically between the fruits of baptism and the fruits of communion[4], there is practically no liturgical expression in the communion order of our having received the Spirit in baptism and so being authorized to approach God with boldness: the congregational recitation of the Lord's prayer becomes, in 1552, a post-communion devotion—quite understandably. It is a powerful and well-organized pattern, and, theologically, has a good deal to be said in its defence: 'all progress in the Christian life depends upon a recapitulation of the original terms of one's acceptance with God (compare Paul's appeals to remember the meaning of being baptized)'.[5] This is important; but it is not self-evident that the *structure* of a communion order should reflect it quite so closely. There is nothing unscriptural in treating the whole eucharistic action, the *doing* of what we are enjoined to do, as a thank-offering: on the contrary, if the blessing or giving of thanks ascribed to Jesus in the earliest narratives is included in what we are to do for his memorial, a eucharist which restricted thanksgiving to the post-communion would be eccentric.[6]

1 Bryan Spinks *Luther's Liturgical Criteria*, p.36.

2 'Good Liturgy or even Good Battlefield?' in *Explorations in Theology*, p.59 (originally in *Theology*, October, 1966).

3 Roger Beckwith and Colin Buchanan, in *Theology*, June 1967, pp.265-271, esp. p.268.

4 See the quotation from his *On the Lord's Supper* in Beckwith and Buchanan, p.268.

5 *Ibid*.

6 Hence I find great difficulty in understanding how Bishop Stephen Neill can say that Cranmer in 1552 'brought together *all* that can be gleaned from the New Testament about the way in which the Eucharist is to be understood' ('Liturgical Continuity and Change in the Anglican Churches' in D. Martin and P. Mullen (eds.) *No Alternative: The Prayer Book Controversy* (Blackwell, London 1981, p.9), *my italics)* —though he makes a valuable point about the 'passover' flavour of 1552.

But this is tilting at windmills in the present liturgical climate: on the whole the centrality of thanksgiving has been pretty universally accepted. The question then is how far this can or should be expressed in sacrificial language and action, and how its relation to the fundamental fact of Calvary can best be articulated. I have argued in this essay for a retrieval of the idea that the effect of Christ's sacrifice is precisely to make us 'liturgical' beings, capable of offering ourselves, our praises and our symbolic gifts to a God who we know will receive us in Christ. Because of the cross we are now directed Godwards 'brought close' (in the root sense of the Semitic *qrb* words) or offered to the Father: what we are is redefined in sacrificial terms—broadly understood. The whole of our worshipping activity is an expression of the reconciliation in the mortal flesh of Christ between God and his creatures. We bring ourselves near to the altar of the cross as we come and offer our gifts—and we are encouraged to do so because the way is open through the flesh of Christ—and are brought to the Father as we claim the fruition of the covenant proclaimed in the paschal event. Through the Spirit's work, the covenant is 'renewed' in us, in our re-entry into the 'sanctuary' of Calvary.

If all this is defensible as an exploration of the basic metaphors of some of our early Christian writers, it should be possible to find some liturgical statement which does justice to the relation between the basic and transforming event of Easter and a real offering to our Father of what he has wrought in us. But the significance of allowing for a language of sacrifice or offering in the eucharist runs deeper. An attitude which resolutely denies that we have anything acceptable to give to God can be far nearer to the anxiety so deprecated by Professor Hanson than would be a more unembarrassed use of sacrificial imagery. We are always in danger (as Heb. 6 reminds us) of *regression* in Christian life: the basic fact of our unqualified dependence on grace can become an alibi, a refusal to assume the authority we in fact have as baptized Christians. The doctrine of salvation as deification has raised many difficulties in Christian history; but part of its justification is to do with the New Testament concern that Christians should understand themselves as heirs of the adult liberty and authority of the firstborn, rather than continuing anxiously to look for an omnipotent Father to provide totally for all needs at every step. We *have been* given, our selves, our Christian selves, as a free gift: to trust God means also to trust ourselves and our worth in his eyes. The haunting image of *Addai and Mari*, of praise offered 'with uncovered faces', speaks volumes about proper Christian self-love. We need to acknowledge that God's gift in making us his children is a *real* gift, and we may do this by trusting his will to receive what we are and what we offer. Our liturgy should celebrate sanctification as well as justification. But the point of continuing to do this in relation to the memorial of Christ's cross is to prevent self-love or self-trust ever becoming uncritical self-assertion: our freedom has a price, our adulthood is not an unproblematic bit of organic growing.

This may help us to see why it is still useful to use the language of sacrifice at all in speaking of worship and eucharist. Don Cupitt has, in his latest book[1], insisted on the intrinsic connection between sacrifice and an

[1] *The World to Come* (London, 1982) p.92.

hierarchical ordering of society: a gift is offered so that favour may be obtained from a superior. But this is to accept a rather simplistic style of anthropological analysis, in which meaning is determined by a highly reductive analysis of supposed 'primitive' practice. J. Van Baal has, as a professional anthropologist, some sharp words for scholars who insist on reducing the act of giving to a simple piece of bribery.[1] For him the small size of certain kinds of traditional ritual offering, substitutes for larger objects, is not an attempt at trickery; what matters about it is *that* it is a gift, and therefore (on his analysis) part of a structure of reciprocity or a system of communication. Both giving and accepting gifts indicates—and sometimes creates—*participation* in a common life or common reality. Sacrifice and offering to the holy thus have to do with the maintenance of fellowship, at the simplest level. Drastic ruptures in harmony may require more drastic means to heal them, but the purpose is always the same. It is worth quoting Van Baal's concluding paragraph:

'True giving is participating, participating in the life and work of the donee, participating in one's universe as a sympathizing member. No one can participate without giving first. Giving is essential for a meaningful existence. The simple food-offering set aside for the gods, the clumsy prayer before meals, and the give-and-take characteristic of mutual care in the small group, are the most real and effective means of communication, cementing togetherness and confirming security. All communication begins with giving, offering.'[2]

In other words, so long as we are concerned with communication, gift, offering, and sacrifice, will continue to be on our agenda. The drama of someone giving up a great deal, perhaps life itself, for the sake of another is appropriately called 'sacrifice' in this perspective because it witnesses to an intense and costly awareness of participation: it is the most extreme demonstration to someone else of his value in your eyes, and so of his share, his stake, in the same world as you.

But there is the difficulty: a gift which creates the profoundest participation involves the profoundest cost. So, on the one hand, God acts, offers, gives, in order to bring creation into fellowship with him; and, because that fellowship is so strange to fearful, self-enclosed, human beings, it requires a uniquely creative gift—a gift which involves God's manifesting himself without power or threat. He 'distances' himself from the stability of his divine life in order to share the vulnerability and darkness of mortal men and women. By the 'gift' of his presence—the presence in our world of an unreserved compassion and an unrestricted hope—he establishes communion; but this can be clearly shown only in conditions of final rejection and dereliction. The gift is consummated on the cross.

So God's gift, which establishes our value and creates a common world, a participation of the divine and the human, involves death. And looked at from the perspective of the man Jesus of Nazareth, there is another kind of

[1] See his essay, 'Offering, sacrifice and gift', in *Numen* vol. *XXIII,* 1976, pp.161-178.
[2] *Ibid.* pp.177-178.

'offering' involved. We look at his life and see in it as a whole God's gift to us, but we can do this only by seeing it at the same time as Jesus' gift to his Father—a 'sacrifice' which will ultimately involve the total loss of a humiliating death. If God's gift to us is consummated on the cross, it is because Jesus' gift to God is so also. It is a gift we cannot give: Christ alone is, to the heart of his being, priest and sacrifice, a man consumed in the fire of Spirit. Only he knows how to glorify the Father in all he does. This is part of what is meant by speaking of his obedience: he is 'consumed' by the Father's will for mercy, grace, reconciliation, because the cost of these in a sinful world is death. He is our acceptable atonement, giving what we cannot give, because he lives and dies in unique nearness to the Holy of Holies, the mercy-seat, the 'propitiatory' place. *Tu solus sanctus;* you alone are consecrated, you alone *belong* in the holy place.

On the other hand: we, drawn into communion, into participation with God through the mutual giving of Jesus and his Father, have become part of a fellowship initiated and sustained by gift, and to abide in this fellowship is to learn how we can give, to each other and to God. That we can give at all rests on what we have *been* given, on the sense of receiving our very selves as gift. Yet we have been shown the cost of giving: the acceptable sacrifice is the one consumed by fire. If we are to be fully a gift to the Father, given by ourselves yet also by and through the crucified Jesus, by our association with that prior gift, we must bear the cost—which is the loss of all we do and all we possess to defend ourselves against God and others and death ('Their fear of fear and frenzy, their fear of possession, of belonging to another, or to others, or to God', wrote Eliot in *East Coker),* against sharing the real vulnerability of the finite world, against the real need and poverty of ourselves and our brothers and sisters. The cost is the loss of images and fantasies, of clear, tight frontiers to the self. If we can even begin to give in this way, it is only because of the depth of the assurance implied in the gift given us on Calvary.

Even the act of praise itself involves a costly giving—not simply the giving up of time[1], but the reorientation of hope and imagination outwards. Praise, celebration. adoration, is a direction away from self-preoccupation, anxiety, defensiveness: like any entry into a wider participation, it demands the yielding of certain protective mechanisms. It is a letting-go of the constant anxious defence of one.s own solidity and worth in order to affirm the worth of something other. What we are talking about is a wide spectrum of human experience, including the decision to sit and absorb a compelling piece of painting or music, and relating to the decision to expose oneself to risk for the sake of a principle, even when immediate practical results are not forthcoming (joining a 'peace camp', demonstrating against religious or ethnic oppression in the Soviet Union, visiting and

[1] 'When a Christian puts aside half an hour of a busy day for the sacrifice of the Mass, he is asserting, to himself as well as to others, that the story of the life, death and resurrection of Christ points to something more profound in his own life than all the flux of opinions, aspirations and regrets, the enjoyment and the tedium, that make up so much of it' (S. Barrington-Ward and M. F. C. Bourdillon, 'A Place for Sacrifice in Modern Christianity' in M. Bourdillon and M. Fortes, (eds.) *Sacrifice,* p.133).

supporting black detainees in South Africa)—all of this focuses on the suspension of our will of defend our safe private territory at all costs. For even that decision to take time for sitting and absorbing is a risky opening of frontiers to what we did not make and do not control. All of it points to the recognition of worth in things or persons irrespective of their immediate use to us—intrinsic value: this is the ground of every act of 'praise' (and this is the sense in which political protest can, as I have suggested, be in some circumstances an act of praise).

And if the reality we confront is self-sufficient, endlessly and unchangingly 'worth-while', then to open ourselves to it in praise is to embark on a project with no imaginable ending, something beyond our power to limit. To be able to praise and adore God worthily is not something instantly and easily accessible: our praise is tied in with the sacrifice, the giving up, of our own sinful and self-protective definition of what we are—and so with the whole act of accepting Christ as the form of the new humanity. And we are drawn to this acceptance by understanding that the new humanity is gift and grace, God sharing himself with his creatures. We come back to the central point of this study: the effect of Christ's offering is to make us capable of offering, to count us worthy to stand and serve as priests.

In instituting a memorial of his death and vindication, his great confirmation of God's ultimate covenant of faithfulness, a covenant now revealed as grounded in his very being, Jesus commands us to reappropriate our new selves in this memorial. We are enjoined to memorialize Easter so that we may enact what we are: the priestly nation of the new covenant. At that level, certainly, it is a remembrance addressed to ourselves, yet it is also the prayer that God may continue to show himself the same God, and in that sense it is a memorial addresssed to him, presented before him—though it is a prayer made in complete confidence that he *is* indeed the God of Easter. All we can really ask is that we should grasp this afresh each day.

'Manward or Godward' is, then, a rather unhelpful dichotomy in thinking about the eucharist. In one sense, *all* our liturgical forms are directed to ourselves, to enable a more fundamental directing of ourselves to God; and of course all liturgical language which purports to 'remind' God of what he is or has done is metaphorical, even mythological. But then the problem affects equally what we can say about the death of Christ. 'Manward'? Yes, because it is nothing if not a pledge and assurance of grace. 'Godward'? Yes, because it is nothing if not the climax of a life directed to the Father. 'Manward' in the sense of a demonstration or an example to follow, and no more? No. 'Godward' in the sense of a blood-offering to change the disposition of a hostile Father? No, in capital letters. Whether we talk of the eucharist or of Calvary, we are deeply involved in myth and metaphor. This certainly does not mean that we cannot speak of an 'objective' atonement; but we do need to acknowledge that 'sacrifice' (as in the New Testament) does not give us any more literal and straightforward a description of our redemption than any other single term. As Van Baal implies, there is even in the simplest rituals of sacrifice an acknowledged element of metaphor: sacrifice is a consciously symbolic act, transferring something (often by the drastic means of killing) from one realm of meaning to another. Only the most bloody-minded of conservative European anthropologists would see it as a 'literal' process of bribery. Wherever we apply the term, metaphor is instantly brought into play. It is a metaphor to talk of thanks and praise, or virtuous life, as a sacrifice; but it is also a metaphor to describe a sordid political execution as a sacrifice. It is a metaphor to describe bread and wine in the eucharist as gifts from God; it is a metaphor to describe the blood of Jesus as a gift for God.

Let me stress again that this is not to obscure necessary distinctions between what we do and what Jesus does, let alone to deny that Jesus, or God in Jesus, does anything at all through the cross. The whole tenor of this paper argues against any such attrition of faith in an effective atonement. But the point is that where we start, where we are on secure ground, is the corporate sense of a renewal of love, freedom, and prayer, and of intimacy with the source of our being and our value, growing out of the story of Jesus' life and death and resurrection: from there on, our language is always exploratory and not always consistent, let alone 'literal' (whatever that means in this context). We think through the experience of renewed humanity in symbols. In a sacrificing culture, the metaphor of sacrifice was peculiarly fruitful, and I have tried in the last few pages to outline how it may still be so even in a non-sacrificing culture: images of gift and loss and participation have not lost their force.

And the metaphor of eucharistic sacrifice depends upon two interacting facts. First (as the comments above on Justin Martyr implied), the ritual *form* of the eucharist was sacrificial—'presenting the gifts', in the familiar and simple phrase of Clement of Rome (Ac Rom. 48). The *Didache* and the *Apostolic Tradition* remind us that gifts other than the eucharistic elements were 'presented' in early Christian practice, but the centrality of this particular offering is beyond dispute. 'The eucharist fulfils all the obvious criteria for sacrifice outlined by the anthropologist.'[1] Second, the eucharist was a memorial of an event which increasingly gathered to itself sacrificial metaphors. It could not be regarded for long by the early church as a pure act of thanksgiving to the Creator (if it ever was; it is more likely that this is a bit of later Gentile rationalization than that it represents a primitive simplicity): it was the offering in which plea was made for the continuing fruits of the foundational 'sacrifice', the authorizing charter for the church's present priestly behaviour and cultic imagery.

We have been quite thoroughly familiarized with the tradition which increasingly sees the body and blood of Christ as passive to the active

---

[1] Adrian Hastings, in a review of Bourdillon and Fortes in *Theology* (September, 1981) p.383. Hastings is rightly critical of the excessive stress on slaughter as essential to sacrifice in the work of many anthropologists, and points out that counter-evidence is to hand in A. Hayley s contribution to the same symposium. His contention that the sacrificial character of the eucharist actually generates the sacrificial interpretation of the cross is intriguing, but ignores the already existing martyrdom-obedience-sacrifice complex in Judaism, and the significance of the Passover context of the crucifixion.

offering of the church (though I do not think Cyprian should be held too guilty on this account: the passage in his *Ep.* 63.14 on the priest's 'imitation, if Christ still stresses the priority of Christ's high priesthood, and the offering '*in* the church').[1] I have tried in these pages to avoid these well-trodden paths, in order to remind the contemporary student, catholic or evangelical, that we are, at least in the earliest period, dealing with an immensely varied and dense cluster of words and pictures—a 'forest of symbols' indeed, in Victor Turner's phrase. The traditions of eucharistic interpretation are multifarious: I am concerned lest a narrow view of what 'sacrifice' means should lead us to ignore a many-layered and suggestive area of symbolism. With many of the criticisms levelled by Professor Hanson against certain ways of talking about the eucharist and their practical and 'political' consequences, I am in entire sympathy; but I do not believe that he (or, indeed, other critics of sacrificial imagery) has told the whole story.

A final point: the style of thinking about eucharistic sacrifice which I have attempted to trace in this essay lends no support to the kind of clericalism which some have associated with the doctrine. On the contrary, it can be seen as a strong statement of the equal dignity of the whole of the new humanity: in Christ, *all* are within the sanctuary, all, ultimately, are brought face to face with the Father (Rev. 22.4), they enter the Holy of Holies. J. M. Ford, in a very valuable paper[2], concludes that this, and the 'bearing' of God's name often spoken of in the Apocalypse, indicates that all the saints are not only priests but high priests (see Ex. 28.26 for the name of God on the high priest's brow): 'they bear the name of Yahweh and stand in his presence, a privilege denied to all save the high priest on the Day of Atonement'.[3] The force of this cultic imagery is to underline the transforming dignity of incorporation into Christ, his work and his self-gift and prayer to the Father.

This is finely put in the last two chapters of C. F. D. Moule's luminous little book on *The Sacrifice of Christ*[4], in which the discussion of eucharistic sacrifice is firmly placed in the context of the 'union of fellowship' (never a 'union of identity') between head and body. The vicarious obedience of Christ is never understood by Christians as a transitory phenomenon belonging to Jesus of Nazareth as an individual: what Christ does he does 'in our place', but it is done in order that we may come to be in his 'place', before the Father. His sacrifice wins a holy people, a praising people, who actualize their priestly task in a uniquely concentrated and fruitful fashion when they offer bread and wine as a memorial and a thanksgiving for the act that still, from moment to moment, consecrates them, secures their access to God. The eucharist is always a celebration of the new humanity, the 'community of gift' between God and human beings and between human beings themselves.

---

[1] See Hanson *op. cit.*, p.19.
[2] 'The Heavenly Jerusalem and Orthodox Judaism' in C. K. Barrett, E. Bammel, W. R. Davies (eds.) *New Testament Studies in honour of David Daube* (Oxford, 1978) pp.214-226.
[3] *Ibid.* p.226.
[4] (London, 1956) pp.31-58, esp. pp.42-55.